# TWISTED GAME OF LIFE

## LIFE AND BEYOND

SUMANTA KUMAR NAYAK

Made with ♥ on the Notion Press Platform
www.notionpress.com

"Dedicated to life, in all its beauty and complexity, may these poems offer a glimpse into its many facets."

# Contents

# Contents

# Preface

I am excited to share this collection of poems "Twisted Game of Life" with you. Each poem in this book reflects my own experiences and observations of the human condition, exploring the many joys and sorrows that we encounter on our journey through life.

Through these poems, I invite you to join me on a journey of self-discovery and reflection. I hope that my words will serve as a reminder that no matter how difficult life may seem, there is always hope and beauty to be found in even the darkest moments.

I believe that poetry has the power to connect us with ourselves and with others, to offer comfort and inspiration, and to shine a light on the complexities of the human experience. I have poured my heart and soul into this collection, and I hope that it will resonate with you and offer a moment of reflection and inspiration.

Thank you for joining me on this journey through the "Twisted Game of Life."

# 1. Twisted Game of Life

Life is a twisted game,
A sadistic joke with a humorous touch.
We laugh and love, then suffer and moan,
As fate plays us like a puppet on a string.
We chase our dreams and cling to hope,
But the reality is a bitter pill to swallow.
We try to make sense of it all,
But the answers elude us like a will-o'-the-wisp.
We search for meaning in the chaos,
But it's a needle in a haystack.
We try to make the best of it,
But the deck is stacked against us.
So we grin and bear it,
With a smile on our faces and a tear in our eyes.
For life is a cruel mistress,
But we love her nonetheless.
We keep on living,
And that's the beauty of it all.
In the end, it's the struggles that make us strong,
And the laughter that keeps us going.

# 2. The Beauty of Contrast: Ice and Fire

Ice and fire, two sides of the same coin,
One brings the chill, the other the scorching heat,
Opposites in nature, yet both so unique,
Both beautiful in their own way, so discreet.
Ice and fire, a contrast of extremes,
One brings the silence, the other the roar,
One stills the mind, the other one teems,
With energy, passion, and so much more.
Ice and fire, a dance of balance,
One brings the cold, the other the flame,
One hardens the earth, the other enhances,
Nature's beauty, never the same.
Ice and fire, a force to be reckoned,
One brings the winter, the other the summer,
One shapes the land, the other protects it,
Together they make life, a wonder.
Ice and fire, a cycle of life,
One brings the death, the other the birth,
Nature's elements, free from strife,
Eternal and constant, on this earth.
Ice and fire, a reminder of the power of nature,
A reminder of the balance we must seek,

To live in harmony with the world around us,
And appreciate the beauty that is unique.
Let us cherish and protect the ice and fire,
That shape our world and make it whole,
For in their presence, we will always find,
A reason to stand in awe, and never grow old.

# 3. Eternal Flame

Life and nature, intertwined,
A dance of balance, always confined.
From the tiniest ant, to the tallest tree,
All are connected, in unity.
Nature's beauty, a sight to behold,
Mountains, oceans, and fields of gold.
The seasons change, with a graceful flow,
And life goes on, a never-ending show.
The sun rises, and sets with grace,
And the stars shine, in the night's embrace.
Nature's rhythms, a melody pure,
A symphony, forever more.
But nature's balance, is fragile too,
Threatened by us, in all we do.
Deforestation, pollution, and waste,
Are destroying, nature's peaceful space.
But life goes on, with a will to survive,
And nature adapts, to stay alive.
We must learn, to live in harmony,
With life and nature, as our destiny.
So let us stand together, hand in hand,
As guardians of this precious land.
Let us work towards a world where nature thrives,

And all living beings can flourish and survive.
So let us cherish, and protect,
Nature's wonders, that we've been blessed with.
For life and nature, are one and the same,
And together, we'll thrive, in eternal flame.

# 4. A Journey of Moments

Eternity of time, a never-ending flow,
A river of moments, forever to go.
Through centuries and ages, it marches on,
A constant reminder of life that has gone.
The past, a memory, etched in our mind,
The future, a mystery, yet to unwind.
But in the present, we find our true selves,
Living in the moment, away from all delves.
Eternity of time, a gift and a curse,
A reminder of life's finite verse.
But in its endless cycle, we find hope,
For tomorrow brings new opportunities to cope.
So let us make the most of every day,
For eternity of time will always find a way.
Let us live, love, and laugh with all our might,
For in the eternity of time, that's our true insight.
Eternity of time, a reminder of our mortality,
A constant companion, on life's journey, it'll be with us eternally.
A reminder to cherish every moment, make it count,
For before we know it, time will pass and our lives amount.
Eternity of time, a witness to history,
A silent observer of humanity's victory and history.

It's seen civilizations rise and fall,
And through it all, time stands tall.
Eternity of time, a teacher of patience,
Showing us that good things come with persistence.
It reminds us that everything happens in its own time,
And that true beauty is found in the climb.
Eternity of time, a mystery to unravel,
A puzzle to solve, a story to unravel.
It's a reminder that life is an ongoing journey,
And that we should cherish it, with all its intensity.
Eternity of time, a never-ending flow,
A river of moments, forever to go.
Let us make the most of every day,
For eternity of time will always find a way.

# 5. A Snowflake's Heart

Innocent and pure, like a freshly fallen snow
A heart untouched by the world's bitter woes
A mind uncluttered, free from care and strife
A spirit untainted by the burdens of life
With eyes that gleam like stars in the night
And a smile that shines so bright and light
A child's laughter echoes like a melody
A symphony of joy, a symphony of glee
Their feet dance to the beat of their own drums
A carefree rhythm, a joyful hum
They run and play, without a care
A wildflower in the field, without a snare
But as they grow and learn of the world's ways
May we not let their innocence fade away
For in their purity, lies our hope and grace
Let us cherish it, always and always.
A bundle of joy, a heart full of trust
A pure and simple soul, free of fuss
Innocent eyes that see the world with wonder
A child's mind, full of dreams to ponder

# 6. Fluid Cosmos

Water, the essence of life,
Flows through the universe, in endless strife.
From the stars to the planets,
Water creates oceans, and it grants
Life to the creatures that call it home,
As it flows and ebbs, it's a cosmic dome.
Water, the giver of birth,
Forms the galaxies, and shapes the earth.
It's in the comets, and in the clouds,
Water, the universe surrounds.
Through the void, it travels far,
In the endless expanse, it's a guiding star.
Water, the mystery of time,
Carries secrets, yet to be mined.
It's in the past, the present, and the future,
Water, the universe's ultimate suture.
As we gaze upon the night sky,
Water reminds us, we are but a tiny cry.
Water, the universe in a drop,
A never-ending cycle, it never stops.
Water, the source of all creation,
Eternity, in its fluid motion.Water, the universe's song,
Echoes forever, in the cosmic throng.

# 7. Whispers in the Night

Darkness, the shadow of the night,
A cloak that covers, a silent blight.
It creeps in slowly, as the sun sets low,
And envelops the world, in its ebony glow.
Darkness, the absence of light,
A mysterious realm, where fears take flight.
It hides secrets, and whispers unknown,
And in its depths, the mind starts to roam.
Darkness, the companion of dreams,
A place where the imagination beams.
It paints pictures, in the mind's eye,
And takes us on journeys, beyond the sky.
Darkness, the friend of the soul,
A place where secrets, it can unfold.
It gives space for introspection,
And allows for self-reflection.
Darkness, the womb of creation,
A place where new ideas take formation.
It gives birth to the stars above,
And the beauty of the universe, to be discovered.
Darkness, the eternal night,
A place where the world takes flight.
It may seem ominous, but in its embrace,

We find peace, and a sense of grace.
So let us not fear the darkness, but instead,
Embrace it with curiosity, and our hearts unfed.
For within its embrace, we can find the light,
And emerge stronger, with newfound sight.

# 8. Shattered Innocence

Innocence lost, in the chaos of war,
A child's laughter, silenced forevermore.
Bombs fall like rain, death all around,
Innocence shattered, on war-torn ground.
Eyes wide with fear, a child's screams,
As death and destruction, their innocence beams.
Homes and families, torn apart,
Innocence sacrificed, for a leader's heart.
Innocence gone, in the face of hate,
War's brutality, a child's fate.
A world of peace, they'll never know,
Innocence stolen, by the war's deadly blow.
But amidst the destruction, a glimmer of hope,
Innocence restored, as humanity begins to cope.
A call for peace, and an end to the fight,
For the innocence of war, to see the light.
As the smoke clears, and the dust settles down,
A new day dawns, with a hopeful sound.
Children's laughter, fills the air,
Innocence restored, with love and care.

# 9. Rainbow's Promise

Rainbows in the sky, a promise of hope,
A reminder of beauty, in the midst of the mope.
A spectrum of colors, a bridge to the divine,
A symbol of love, that will always shine.
The spirit of the rainbow, a reminder to dream,
A guide on the journey, to our hearts supreme.
It reminds us to see the world with new eyes,
And to find the beauty, in the big and small ties.
The spirit of the rainbow, is a call to be bold,
To chase our passions, and break from the mold.
It reminds us to be true to ourselves,
And to find the courage, to be someone else.
The spirit of the rainbow, is a light in the dark,
A reminder that, love will always spark.
So let us embrace, the spirit of the rainbow,
And let it guide us, wherever we may go.
For the spirit of the rainbow, is a beacon of light,
Guiding us through the darkest of night.
So let us embrace, its beauty and grace,
And let it fill us with hope, in every single space.

# 10. Guiding Lights

Lovable parents, with hearts of gold,
Wisdom flowing, through young and old.
They guide us through, the trials and strife,
With love and patience, in their very life.
With open minds, they see the world anew,
Each day a canvas, to paint and imbue.
Their passions spark, a fire in our hearts,
And we are inspired, to make our own art.
They encourage us, to chase our dreams,
With gentle nudges, and loving schemes.
Their words of wisdom, ring in our ears,
As we face the future, with no more fears.
Lovable parents, we are blessed,
To have you in our lives, we are possessed.
With your guidance, we'll soar so high,
And reach for the stars, in the endless sky.
Thank you, dear parents, for all you've done,
For the love and support, you've shown every one.
We'll cherish the memories, forevermore,
And be grateful, for the lovable parents, we adore.

# 11. Chaos and Hope

Is humanity in danger, as we look around,
A world of chaos, with no peace to be found.
Wars and famine, disease and hate,
A constant struggle, to keep our fate.
Nature's fury, unleashed on our land,
Climate change, a threat we can't withstand.
Pollution choking, our oceans and skies,
A bleak future, before our eyes.
Hatred and bigotry, tearing us apart,
Equality and justice, a dream to start.
The divisions are deep, the wounds are raw,
As we struggle to find, a common cause.
But hope still lingers, in the darkest hour,
For humanity is strong, and has the power.
To come together, and make a change,
To heal the wounds, and rearrange.
The future is uncertain, but one thing is true,
We have the ability, to shape it anew.
With love and compassion, we can mend,
And save humanity, till the very end.

# 12. Small But Mighty

Small and insignificant,
A creature often overlooked,
But this ant, with its antenna, bent,
Is content and happy, never mistook.
It scurries along the ground,
With purpose and a steady pace,
Carrying its burden around,
With a smile upon its face.
It may not have grand ambitions,
Or a life filled with luxury,
But it's content with its conditions,
And finds joy in its simplicity.
It may not be a ruler or a king,
But it's a part of something grand,
A member of a bustling team,
Working together hand in hand.
So let us all take a cue,
From this happy little ant,
And find contentment in the simple things we do,
And make the most of what we've got.

# 13. The Double-Edged Sword

Power, a force that can make or break,
A thing of beauty or a heart's mistake.
It flows through kings and peasants alike,
A river that can either nourish or spike.
In the hands of the wise, it brings peace and light,
In the hands of the foolish, it brings only blight.
It can lift the oppressed and bring down the proud,
It can make the weak strong, and the strong bowed.
It can bring forth progress and change the world,
Or it can fuel greed and make it unfurled.
It can be used for good or used for ill,
A tool that we must learn to wield with skill.
Power, a thing we all possess,
To use it well, we must always assess.
For true power lies not in might,
But in the will to make things right.
To use it justly, with wisdom and grace,
To lift others up and make the world a better place.
To see beyond ourselves and our own gain,
To use our power for the greater good, without refrain.

# 14. Timeless Tango

Earth and moon, two celestial spheres,
In orbit, they dance without any fears.
Earth, a blue and green canvas of life,
Moon, a pale and glowing orb, a silent wife.
Earth spins on its axis, day and night,
Moon circles round, reflecting Earth's light.
Earth's oceans ebb and flow with the tide,
Moon's craters and mountains, a story to confide.
Earth, home to diverse creatures and plants,
Moon, a barren and lifeless place, but it still grants
Earth with its phases, a guide for time,
Moon, a companion for Earth, a cosmic chime.
Earth and moon, two bodies in space,
Inseparable, they share a cosmic grace.
Earth, a living being, Moon, a dead rock,
Together, they form a beautiful clock.
The dance between Earth and moon is a timeless tango,
A cosmic symphony, a bond that forever flows.
Two celestial spheres in sync they sway,
Fearless in their orbit, they move in cosmic play.

# 15. Cosmic Companion

A shining star in the night sky,
A beacon of hope, a guiding light.
It twinkles and glows with a steady shine,
A reminder of beauty, a cosmic sign.
A shining star, a symbol of dreams,
A guide to follow, a path it beams.
It illuminates the darkest night,
With its radiant light, it sets things right.
A shining star, a companion in the journey,
A light in the distance, a source of comfort and safety.
It shines through the storms, and guides us home,
A shining star, never to be alone.
A shining star, a messenger of fate,
A sign of good luck, a destiny to create.
It shines with a purpose, a destiny to fulfill,
A shining star, a story to thrill.
A shing star, a symbol of hope,
A light in the darkness, a way to cope.
It's a reminder that in the vastness of space,
We're never alone, with a shining star to grace.
A shining star, a beauty to behold,
A cosmic wonder, a story to be told.
It's a reminder of the vastness of the universe,

And the infinite possibilities that lie ahead, in its verse.
A shining star, a beacon of light,
A bridge between worlds, a path to insight.
It holds the secrets of the universe within,
A cosmic treasure trove, waiting to begin.

# 16. Joy's Overflow

Tears of happiness, a bittersweet release,
A sign of joy, a heart at peace.
A welling up of emotion, a flood of delight,
A feeling so pure, it brings tears to sight.
With each droplet that falls, a weight is lifted,
The soul feels renewed, the spirit is gifted.
It's a moment of gratitude, a moment of grace,
As we bask in the warmth of love's embrace.
Tears of happiness, a language of the heart,
A way to express what words cannot impart.
It's a release of all that's held inside,
A floodgate of feelings, that cannot be denied.
So let the tears flow, in all their glory,
For they're a sign of a life's true story.
A testament to the human heart,
And the beauty that lies within its art.
Tears of happiness, a reminder of life's worth,
A celebration of all that we hold dear on earth.
So cherish the moments that bring tears to your eyes,
For they're a reminder of life's endless surprise.

# 17. A Journey Through Time

Time flows like a river, ceaseless and swift
And we are but mere passengers on its drift
It carries us forward, through joy and strife
And marks each moment of our fleeting life.
The first steps we take, so tentative and small
Soon turn into strides, as we learn to walk tall
Childhood days fly by, filled with laughter and play
But before we know it, they have slipped away.
Adolescence beckons, with its thrills and fears
As we search for our place in this world, with tears
Time marches on, never slowing its pace
As we navigate the twists and turns of life's race.
The bloom of youth fades, giving way to age
As we face the truth of our mortality, engaged
In a struggle to hold onto what's dear
As time's steady march becomes ever more clear.
Yet, in the midst of this journey we take
There are moments of beauty that cause us to wake
And cherish the memories that we have made
As we reflect on the passage of time, and how it has shaped.
For though time's unrelenting flow may seem cruel
It has a way of enriching us, making us jewels

In the crown of existence, with our unique hue
A testament to the ways time has brought us through.
So let us embrace each moment, cherish it well
For we cannot know when time will toll its final bell
And may we look back on a life fully lived
With the passage of time, a gift that we give.

# 18. Wandering Soul

I wandered down a path, one bright summer's day
Not knowing where it led, or what lay on the way
But something in me stirred and whispered in my ear
"Come, wanderer, come - there is much to discover here."
And so I followed that path, with eagerness and hope
Through fields of golden wheat, and up a wooded slope
I climbed a mountain's peak and watched the world below
And felt a sense of wonder, that only travelers know.
I met strangers on my journey, who became friends so true
And shared with them my stories, and heard their tales anew
Together we walked on, through valleys and through hills
Finding beauty in the journey, and strength in all its thrills.
I faced my fears and doubts, as the road grew rough and steep
And learned to trust myself, even when I felt weak
For every challenge on the path, brought growth and transformation
And showed me new dimensions, in the landscape of creation.
And when at last the journey ended, and I reached my destination
I felt a sense of wonder and deep appreciation
For all that I had learned, and all the memories made
And knew that I'd been changed, by the journey I had braved.

For every journey, we embark on, be it near or far
Brings us closer to our truth, and who we truly are
So may we embrace the wanderer within, and follow where it leads
For in the journey of life, we find our greatest needs.
And though the path may wind, and twist and turn along the way
And though we may stumble, and falter, and lose our way
The wanderer within us, will always guide us true
To find the path that's meant for us, and all that we can do.
So let us wander down the paths, that beckon us to go
With open hearts and minds, and the courage to let go
Of all that holds us back, and keeps us from our dreams
For in the journey of life, is where true magic gleams.
And when the journey's over, and we've reached the end of days
May we look back with joy, on all the winding ways
For in the journey of life, we find our greatest needs
And in the wanderer's heart, we find the strength to succeed.

# 19. A Symphony in Green

Green, oh wondrous green,
Your hue so rich, your tone so clean,
A symbol of life, of growth, of hope,
A color that helps the weary to cope.
When I see you, my heart fills with peace,
As if all the troubles in the world do cease,
You remind me of the forest and the trees,
Of a quiet place where I can be at ease.
Your verdant hue is like a balm,
Calming the senses, bringing a sense of calm,
You speak of new beginnings, of things that grow,
Of the potential that lies within us, waiting to show.
You are the color of nature, of balance, and of health,
A symbol of all that is pure, of all that is felt,
You bring to mind fields of clover, and leaves of mint,
A freshness, a clarity, a sense of being in sync.
Green, you are the color of spring,
Of the season of rebirth, when all is beginning,
You speak to the soul, of things yet to come,
Of possibilities, and of journeys to be begun.
In your presence, I find a sense of renewal,
A promise of things to come, a chance to be true,
For green, you are the color of life, of vitality,

A symbol of all that we can be, and all that we can see.
Green, oh wondrous green,
You are a sight to be seen,
A color that brings peace and calm,
A hue that can be like a soothing balm.

# 20. A Summer Afternoon in Childhood

As I close my eyes and reminisce,
A childhood memory I cannot dismiss,
A time when life was carefree and light,
And the world seemed to be all right.
It was a day of pure delight,
A summer afternoon, so warm and bright,
When the sun was high up in the sky,
And I felt as if I could touch it if I tried.
I was playing in my backyard, all alone,
With my favorite toy, a frisbee, thrown,
Tossing it high up in the air,
And catching it, without a single care.
The grass was soft, the breeze was cool,
And I felt like I was swimming in a pool,
Of endless joy, and boundless fun,
Under the warm embrace of the sun.
But then, something caught my eye,
And I looked up to the clear blue sky,
To see a flock of birds, flying so high,
In a perfect formation, like a painting in the sky.
I watched them for what felt like hours,
Mesmerized by their synchronized powers,

And I felt a sense of awe and wonder,
As if I had stumbled upon a hidden treasure.
And in that moment, I felt so free,
As if the whole world was just for me,
A child, innocent, and full of glee,
With nothing to worry, and nothing to be.
That childhood memory still sticks with me,
A precious gem, a treasure, so free,
A time of joy, and of endless fun,
Under the warm embrace of the sun.

# 21. Alone but Not Lonely

The world is a vast and wondrous place,
Full of beauty, wonder, and grace,
And though we share this planet fair,
Each journey we take is ours to bear.
For there's a magic in solo travel,
A sense of freedom, and of marvel,
That comes when we strike out alone,
To places we've never known.
There's a certain joy in being free,
To chart our own path, to just be,
To wander aimlessly, or have a plan,
To explore a new world, as only we can.
We learn to trust ourselves, our inner voice,
To make choices, and to rejoice,
In the wonder of discovery,
As we journey to the ends of the earth, quite literally.
We meet strangers who become friends,
And learn to see the world through different lens,
To hear new stories, and to share our own,
To break down barriers, and feel less alone.
There's a power in solitude,
A chance to reflect, and to renew,
To find inner peace, and clarity,

In the midst of all life's uncertainty.
For when we travel solo, we can see,
The world and ourselves more honestly,
And find new depths of understanding,
Of who we are, and where we're standing.
So let us embrace the essence of solo travel,
And let our spirits and hearts unravel,
In the beauty of a world so vast and bright,
A journey that brings us closer to the light.

# 22. Nature's Symphony

Amidst the beauty of the world, we see,
There's much to cherish, much to believe,
Nature's symphony, with every beat,
A source of peace, a harmony, so sweet.
As the sun sets beyond the horizon's line,
A canvas of colors, a masterpiece divine,
The sky ignites with hues of red and gold,
A sight to behold, so grand and bold.
And in a field of flowers, a single bloom,
A rose so rare, with sweet perfume,
Its petals soft, with shades of pink,
A fragile beauty, that makes us think.
And when a storm rages, with its fierce might,
With thunder's boom, and lightning's light,
A show of nature's strength and power,
An awe-inspiring, breathtaking shower.
Yet through it all, there's a beauty that's rare,
A connection, a balance, that's always there,
A reminder of nature's infinite grace,
A harmony that weaves through time and space.
For nature's beauty is beyond compare,
A sight, a sound, that's everywhere,
In every sunset, flower, and storm,

A wonder to behold, a true reform.
So let us cherish each moment, every day,
And take a moment to breathe and say,
Thank you, nature, for all you give,
For the beauty and wonder in which we live.

# 23. The Power of Kindness: Atithi Devo Bhava

Hindu culture, so rich and old,
A tapestry of stories and beliefs told,
A way of life, that's steeped in tradition,
A source of hope, and divine rendition.
It's a culture that embraces humanity,
And celebrates diversity in all its beauty,
It teaches us to love, to give, to share,
To seek the write a poem on "atithi devo bhawa"
Atithi Devo Bhava, a Sanskrit phrase,
A sacred belief, a culture we praise,
It means "Guest is God," a guiding light,
To treat each visitor with love and delight.
In India, where hospitality reigns,
This philosophy, our hearts maintain,
A tradition passed down through the years,
To honor guests with respect and cheers.
No matter the guest, their caste or creed,
We welcome them with love and proceed,
To offer them food, shelter, and care,
To treat them with kindness, with love, and with prayer.

We see divinity in every guest,
And serve them with joy and our very best,
To make them feel welcomed and at ease,
And leave with memories that forever please.
For Atithi Devo Bhava is more than just a phrase,
It's a way of life, a culture we embrace,
It shows us that humanity is the key,
To treat each other with love and dignity.
So let us continue this ancient way,
To treat each guest like God, every day,
To show kindness, respect, and love,
And honor the divine in all, above.

# 24. Dancing in the Rain

I love rain, oh how it falls,
A symphony of nature, a gift to all,
Each drop, a messenger of peace,
A rhythm that brings my soul release.
The patter of raindrops on the ground,
A calming sound, so serene and profound,
The smell of wet earth, so fresh and sweet,
A fragrance that makes my heart skip a beat.
The rain washes away the dust and grime,
Leaves everything anew, so clean and divine,
It nourishes the earth, and brings new life,
A source of hope, in the midst of strife.
I love to dance, in the pouring rain,
To feel the drops, on my face, again and again,
To sing out loud, with the thunder's roar,
And embrace the moment, forevermore.
The rain reminds me, of love and grace,
And the beauty that surrounds us in every place,
It brings a peace, that words can't express,
A wonder, a joy, that we must confess.
The rain brings a sense of calm,
And washes away our worries and qualms,
It cleanses our souls, and sets us free,

A blessing from above, for all to see.
So let the rain fall, let it pour,
For it's a gift that we should adore,
A reminder of life, and love, and more,
A symphony of nature, that we should explore.

# 25. The Battle Within

Within each of us, a battle rages on,
A war between two realms, never gone,
Hell and heaven, two sides of a coin,
A struggle that defines how we will join.
Deep inside, where the heart beats strong,
A tug of war that's been going on too long,
A battle for control, a fight for peace,
A quest to find the light, the pain to ease.
Hell, with its flames, and its heat,
A place where agony and pain meet,
A world of darkness, where fear prevails,
And anger and hate, forever trails.
Heaven, a place of light and love,
Where grace descends from above,
A world of peace, where hope prevails,
And kindness and compassion, forever trails.
The war within, a choice we must make,
Which path to take, which side to undertake,
To walk in the light or descend into the dark,
To choose the right or follow the mark.
The battle rages on, each and every day,
A quest to find the light, a new way,
To let go of the darkness, and embrace the light,

To find our way home, and leave behind the night.
So let us choose, the path we take,
And strive for love, and give hate a break,
To heal our wounds, and find our way,
To live in the light, and find the day.

Printed by Libri Plureos GmbH in Hamburg, Germany